QUESTIONS TO RULE THE WORLD

Questions to Rule the World

Challenge the Old
Embrace the New
Achieve Next-Level
Success

SOPHIE KRANTZ

Sophie Krantz

CONTENTS

INTRODUCTION

SECTION 1: THE STATUS QUO

SECTION 2: WHAT MATTERS MOST TO YOU

SECTION 3: THE ACTION YOU'LL TAKE TO ACHIEVE
NEXT-LEVEL SUCCESS

CONCLUSION

Published by Sophie Krantz

First published in 2024 in Melbourne, Australia

Copyright © Sophie Krantz

www.sophiekrantz.com

ISBN 978-1-7635976-2-4 (paperback)

ISBN 978-1-7635976-3-1 (ebook)

The moral rights of the author have been asserted.

To those who question what they can build and achieve in the world: may you explore, experiment, and expand in a universe of possibilities.

INTRODUCTION

Questora. That was my codename in the mobile phone of the head of security at a European airline during my early 20s, while I was on a working holiday in Italy. I earned this nickname due to my relentless questioning about the what, how, and why of things. This deep curiosity has significantly shaped my approach to global business strategy. As the world continues to evolve rapidly, I believe the need for such curiosity — the sense that there is always more to understand and create — has never been more important.

Questions wield immense power. They shape our understanding, drive innovation, and challenge the status quo. Leading academics underscore the importance of questioning as a tool for learning and discovery. Albert Einstein famously encouraged, "*The important thing is not to stop questioning. Curiosity has its own reason for existing.*" Similarly, Rainer Maria Rilke advised, "*Live your questions now, and perhaps even without knowing it, you will live along some distant day into your answers.*"

The Shift from Industrial to Digital. We are witnessing a significant shift from the slow, steady nature of the Industrial Age to the rapid, interconnected dynamics of the Digital Era. In the past, businesses could rely on long-term planning and incremental improvements. Today, digital technology accelerates change, dissolves barriers, and intensifies the interconnectedness of global markets. This new era demands agility, foresight, and a readiness to embrace uncertainty. Leaders must now navigate a landscape where change is the only constant, and opportunities or challenges can arise globally with unprecedented speed.

Why Rule the World? Today's rapid evolution from the Industrial Age's steady pace to the fast, interconnected Digital Era presents an imporant shift for leaders. The urgency for agility, foresight, and

2

embracing uncertainty has never been greater. This book guides leaders to shift beyond conventional limits and foster sustainable, win-win outcomes that benefit societies globally while building next, needed, better products, services, and businesses. It empowers you to challenge existing paradigms, embrace transformative opportunities, and lead with a vision that extends beyond mere profit, aiming for impactful, inclusive success on a global stage.

Confronting the Status Quo. Our perception and leadership in the world can become constrained if they are solely moulded by negative news, a dominant narrative that discourages deviation from the status quo, or uninspired leadership models. Educational biases, echo chambers in social or professional networks, and limited exposure to diverse cultures and ideas further constrict our view, confining our thinking to a local or narrow scope. This limitation restricts our ability to envision broader possibilities and seize diverse or global opportunities.

There's more to the world than what we see. Shifting our perspective shapes what we can achieve. Beyond our lived experiences — of who we know, what we know, and how we work — lies a world of possibility. It is beneficial to refresh our worldview and interpret it anew.

The questions in this book are crafted to reflect on the external world and to also explore deeply your internal motivations and aspirations. They aim to connect you with what truly matters — to you, your team, and your organisation. This book is designed to unlock your potential and guide you toward a definition of next-level success that is both sustainable and adaptable, tailored to the evolving landscapes of technology and market conditions. This success is future-oriented, aiming for greater achievements than your current standing.

Each question serves as an invitation to expansive thinking, challenging you to consider scenarios that stretch beyond the conventional and provoke transformative thought.

The world is tumultuous. For those of us with years, or even decades ahead in our professional lives, it is crucial to move beyond the examples set on the current world stage. As we face economic downturns, environmental crises, and widespread conflicts, breaking away from conventional approaches may be essential to achieving both commercial and leadership success, as well as the transformative outcomes our times demand.

We often question the external world — leadership, policies, business models. Yet, perhaps the most critical questions are those that are internal, determining what matters most to us. What has the potential to shift our focus and shape our path to achieve next-level success?

When we focus on what matters and align this with who we know, what we know, and how we work, a world of possibility opens up.

Does your worldview inspire, instruct, and influence your next-level success? This book aims to do just that for you, your team, and your organisation.

The book is structured into three sections:

- **Section 1: The Status Quo** - This section delves into the current state of affairs, examining established norms, conventional wisdom, and traditional business practices. It encourages you to critically evaluate the status quo and identify outdated methods and beliefs that could hinder innovation and growth.
- **Section 2: What Matters Most to You** - This section focuses on introspection and personal values. It guides you through understanding what truly matters to you and your organisation, aligning your strategies and actions with your core values.
- **Section 3: The Action You'll Take to Achieve Next-Level Success** - The final section translates insights into action. You will zoom-out, to think as far and wide as possible, in order to strategically zero-in on who you need to know, what you need to know, and how you work. This section provides a framework

for developing actionable strategies that leverage your under-standing of the status quo and your core values while setting ambitious goals.

How to Use This Book:

- **Team Discussions:** Use each question as a starting point for team meetings or strategy sessions. A single question can open up a broad discussion and lead to unexpected insights and inno-vative solutions.
- **Personal Reflection:** Reflect on these questions in your per-sonal time to deeply understand your own leadership style, busi-ness approach, and the broader impact of your decisions.
- **Thought Experiments:** Conduct thought experiments by ex-ploring hypothetical scenarios based on each question. This can help anticipate challenges and imagine new possibilities.
- **Leadership Workshops:** Incorporate these questions into lead-ership development workshops or retreats as a way to challenge and grow emerging leaders within your organisation.
- **Journaling:** Use the questions for journaling to track your thoughts and progress over time. This can be an effective way to document insights and develop a clearer vision for the future.

It's perfectly normal if you find some questions challenging or if you don't have immediate answers. This indicates areas where there may be gaps in awareness or capability that could be crucial for achieving next-level success. Embrace these gaps as opportunities for growth and learning.

This book is intended to be flexible in its use, adaptable to your spe-cific needs and context. Whether you progress through it sequentially or jump around to sections that are most pertinent at the moment, the goal is to inspire and provoke — a tool to help you rule your world, however you define it.

Let these questions be the catalyst for change and innovation in your leadership journey, pushing you to think bigger and act bolder.

Let's challenge the old and embrace the new together.

SECTION 1: THE STATUS QUO

1. What aspects of your industry are currently under the most strain, and why?

2. If the leading player in your market suddenly ceased operations, how would you adapt your strategy?

3. Identify a practice within your industry that might become obsolete in the next ten years. What would replace it?

4. What vulnerabilities in your industry could a well-funded new-comer exploit?

5. How resilient is your business to changes in technology? Would you survive if the dominant tech became obsolete overnight?

6. What is the secret behind your success? If you lost all tangible assets, what remains?

7. Which of your products or services is least aligned with current market trends and customer preferences?

8. How would your operations adjust to a complete disruption of global supply chains?

9. What regulations pose the greatest challenge to your current operational model, and how could these potentially change?

10. How effectively does your current business model handle sudden market shifts or disruptions?

11. If you had to phase out one of your departments or product lines immediately, which would it be and what would be the implications?

12. Consider the impact of a shift from a product-based to a service-based business model. What steps would you need to take?

13. What opportunities would arise for your business if the primary external threat to your industry disappeared tomorrow?

14. How would a halving of production costs change your industry? What strategic moves would you make?

15. If consumer preferences shifted entirely towards sustainability, how would you realign your business to meet these demands?

16.Evaluate the response of your industry to recent global crises. What lessons can you draw from these reactions?

17. Imagine your company had to achieve zero carbon emissions by next year. Outline the initial steps you would take to start this transition.

18. How would your company react if stricter data privacy regulations were immediately enforced?

19. What would your response be if your main product line was suddenly considered unsafe or unhealthy within the next 30 days?

20. How would you respond to a sudden demographic shift in your target market?

21. Explore alternative materials or processes you could use if there was an instant ban on your most used raw material.

22. How would a shift in policy that makes a lesser market more lucrative affect your strategic priorities?

23. What would be your strategy if a crucial foreign market you depend on suddenly became inaccessible?

24. Plan your response to a hypothetical invalidation of a key patent your business relies on.

25. How would heavy internet regulation impact your digital strategy?

26. What contingency plans would you implement if a major supplier suddenly went bankrupt?

27. If you could merge with any company globally, who would it be and what strategic advantages would you gain?

28. Describe how you would transition to a completely circular economy model within your business.

29. What changes would you make if AI could automate your main service?

30. How would you adapt if your consumer base suddenly aged by 20 years?

31. Identify a profitable niche market within your industry. How would you approach this market?

32. Outline the changes you would implement if your business had to operate entirely remotely.

33. How would you take advantage of your biggest competitor exiting the market?

SECTION 2: WHAT MATTERS MOST TO YOU

34. If you could change one aspect of your company culture overnight, what would it be and why?

35. What if you had to start your business from scratch today; what core value would you build it around?

36. Imagine your business has achieved your ultimate goal; what does this success look like?

37. If you could solve one problem affecting your industry, what would it be and how would it align with your personal values?

38. How would you redesign your business if employee well-being and environmental impact were your top priorities?

39. What if your current target market no longer exists; which new demographic would you focus on?

40. Envision your company has unlimited resources; where would you invest first to make the most significant impact?

41. If a major public scandal affected your industry, how would you use this as an opportunity to lead by example?

42. What if the biggest internal resistance within your company dissolved; what change would you implement immediately?

43. If you could only keep one leadership trait, what would it be and why?

44. What would you prioritise if your company could only focus on one strategic objective next year?

45. If a global study found your main product to be the most desired item, how would you exploit this fame?

46. Imagine you received an award for leadership in sustainability; what actions would have earned you this?

47. What if you had to integrate an entirely new technology into your product; how would you ensure it aligns with user needs?

48. How would your decision-making process change if your company became publicly traded?

49. What if you could influence global industry standards; what standards would you set?

50. Imagine you had to advise a startup in your field; what ethical practices would you emphasise?

51. What if your business had the chance to lead a global movement; what cause would you champion?

52. How could you modify your product line to better reflect your commitment to diversity and inclusion?

53. What if you had the power to change one law that affects your business; what would you change and why?

54. Imagine your business model is used as a case study in business schools; what lessons would you want to highlight?

55. What if you had to write a mission statement that included corporate social responsibility; what would it say?

56. How would you redesign your customer service to truly reflect your company's values?

57. What if you could start a foundation or charity as part of your business; what would be its mission? How would you measure its impact?

58. Imagine you had an unlimited budget for a marketing campaign; how would it reflect what truly matters to your brand?

59. If you were to retire tomorrow, what values would you want to remain as your legacy in the company?

60. What if you could change the industry perception of your company overnight; what would you want it to be known for?

61. How would you redefine success for your business beyond financial metrics?

62. What if you could eliminate one major stressor for your employees; what would it be and how would it improve company culture?

63. Imagine your business as a leader in customer trust; what practices would have built this reputation?

64. How would you structure your company if mental health and physical wellness were the top priorities?

65. What if your personal values were misaligned with your company's actions; how would you realign them?

66. Imagine you had to create a company manifesto that all employees must follow; what key points would it include?

SECTION 3: THE ACTION YOU'LL TAKE TO ACHIEVE NEXT-LEVEL SUCCESS

67. If a tech giant CEO could work for you for a day, how would you utilise their expertise to instigate a significant transformation in your business operations, strategy, or business model?

68. Imagine having Apple's design team for a week; what ground-breaking product or feature would you direct them to develop that aligns uniquely with your company's future vision?

69. If invited to a global summit with world leaders, what transformative policy or idea would you advocate for that could potentially reshape global industry standards or address major societal challenges?

70. How could AI be integrated across your business operations to enhance productivity and create new user experiences or open up new markets?

71. Envision forming an elite advisory network from across the globe; who are the six individuals you would choose, and how would their specific expertise propel your strategic goals?

72. Where in the world is untapped talent located that could drive next-level growth for your business? How would you engage with this talent pool?

73. If you received a sudden influx of $1 billion, how would you allocate this investment to maximise impact and return?

74. If you had a dedicated team of AI specialists for a month, what groundbreaking project would you have them work on that could revolutionise aspects of your business or industry?

75. With access to a private jet for a week, which global hotspots would you visit and which key stakeholders or potential partners would you meet to expand your business horizons?

76. Imagine raising $1 million in one hour; what compelling message or unique value proposition would enable this remarkable funding achievement?

77. If you committed to launching one new experiment each month for the next year to stay closer to your market, what types of experiments would these be and what key hypotheses would you test?

78. What is the single most crucial piece of strategic intelligence that could significantly influence your company's market positioning or competitive advantage?

79. From whom could you obtain strategic intelligence more swiftly and effectively than your competitors, and how could this information be utilised to forge a competitive edge?

80. If you could redefine one core process within your company using cutting-edge technology, what process would it be and what technology would you use?

81. How would you leverage global trends in sustainability and corporate responsibility to enhance your brand reputation and also drive tangible business benefits?

82. What strategic partnerships could you form that would dramatically accelerate your entry into new markets or sectors?

83. If you could implement one policy change in your industry that would benefit your company strategically, what would it be and how would you advocate for it?

84. What would you do differently if you knew there was no chance of failure in expanding your business globally?

85. How can you use virtual reality to simulate and explore new business models or improve customer engagement?

86. If you could integrate one futuristic technology into your products or services today, what would it be, and how would it transform your customer experience or operational efficiency?

87. If you could shadow a global leader for a week, who would it be and what insights would you hope to gain?

88. Imagine you could redesign your business model with a focus on zero waste; what steps would you take to achieve this?

89. How would you use blockchain technology to enhance transparency and trust within your business operations?

90. What new market could you enter if logistical constraints were no longer a barrier, and how would you go about it?

91. If you could collaborate with any artist or creative thinker to revamp your brand, who would it be and what unique elements would they bring?

92. What if you could launch a satellite to improve a particular aspect of your business; what function would it serve?

93. How would you harness the power of crowd-sourcing to solve a critical challenge your company faces?

94. What game-changing product could you develop if you collaborated with a leading tech company?

95. If you had to build a new headquarters in a location that best represents your company's future, where would it be and why?

96. Imagine you could start a new venture tomorrow in a completely different industry; what would it be and what would you bring from your current experience?

97. If global travel restrictions permanently changed, how would you restructure your business for maximum efficiency and reach?

98. What if you could end one global problem with your company's resources; which would you tackle and how?

99. If you had a futurist on your team for a year, what specific projects or strategic objectives would you assign them to maximise their impact on your organization's future readiness?

100. **What if you ruled the world?** Imagine possessing the power to shape global markets, influence international policies, establish environmental standards, and solve a socioeconomic issue at your discretion. How would you wield this authority to create positive changes in your company and for the planet?

CONCLUSION

As we draw *Questions to Rule the World: Challenge the Old, Embrace the New, Achieve Next-Level Success* to a close, we are reminded of the transformative power of inquiry in driving change and innovation. This book has been crafted to instil a curiosity that is as relentless in its pursuit of knowledge and understanding as it is in its quest for innovative solutions.

Reflecting on the Journey. Throughout this book, we have engaged with questions that challenge us to rethink outdated practices and embrace new paradigms. From questioning the efficacy of long-standing business models to exploring the potential of emerging technologies, each query has been designed to spur critical thinking and innovative solutions. Inspired by the words of Indian philosopher Jiddu Krishnamurti, "*The ability to observe without evaluating is the highest form of intelligence.*" This book encourages such observation; it prompts us to look at the familiar in unfamiliar ways, to question what we believe we know, and to remain open to new perspectives.

Why We Challenge The Old. By daring to question the old, we unlock the potential to shed restrictive practices that limit creativity and stifle innovation. This book has encouraged you to scrutinise the conventional frameworks that no longer suffice in today's fast-paced, complex global environment. In doing so, it invites more adaptive, inclusive, and effective strategies to surface, allowing us to navigate the challenges of an increasingly interconnected world.

Why We Embrace The New. Embracing the new is crucial for thriving in the digital age and a time of worldwide shifts in economic and geopolitical power. This involves adopting new technologies and also rethinking leadership styles and business strategies to align with modern realities. The discussions and explorations prompted by this book are intended to position you at the forefront of your field, ensuring that your approaches are progressive and trailblazing.

Why We Aim for Next-Level Success. Achieving next-level success involves crafting strategies that create positive outcomes for all stakeholders, moving beyond the zero-sum game to a more holistic, win-win approach. This book champions such strategies, advocating for business practices that contribute positively to society while ensuring robust economic growth.

The Road Ahead. As you continue to navigate your leadership path, let the questions posed in this book guide your strategic decisions. Revisit them regularly to inspire team discussions, inform leadership workshops, and adapt to new challenges as both you and your business evolve.

Questions to Rule the World is a collection of questions and it is a manifesto for continuous exploration, experimentation, and expansion. It champions a curious and critical mindset that constantly seeks deeper understanding and never settles for easy answers. Whether used to ignite debates, guide deep reflections, or inspire groundbreaking innovations, the ultimate goal remains the same: to empower you to redefine success on your own terms and lead transformation in your sphere.

Thank you for joining this journey of transformation. As we collectively challenge the old and embrace the new, let us strive towards achieving next-level success together. Let these questions be your catalyst for change, inspiring you to think bigger, act bolder, and shape a future where everyone can thrive.

Sophie Krantz is a global strategist who specializes in guiding business leaders, entrepreneurs, and changemakers through complex and disruptive market environments. Over the last two decades, she has successfully managed international business expansion projects in 23 countries, with project values of up to US$1 billion. Her experience spans multiple senior roles in Global Fortune 500 and ASX200 companies across industries such as financial services and advanced manufacturing.

Sophie's expertise also extends to her work with the International Trade Centre, the joint agency of the United Nations and World Trade Organization, where she spearheaded trade and investment strategies aimed at fostering economic growth in low and middle-income countries. As a certified practitioner of the Exponential Organization framework, Sophie collaborates with Global Fortune 2000 companies to update and expand their business models by incorporating strategies used by the world's fastest-growing companies. She guides leaders and organisations in thinking, acting, and leading globally.

To learn more about Sophie's work, visit www.sophiekrantz.com.

www.ingramcontent.com/pod-product-compliance
Lightning Source LLC
Chambersburg PA
CBHW041208220326
41597CB00030BA/5128